STEAM ON THE SOUTH WESTERN
A Colour Portfolio

R. C. Riley

Ian Allan
60th
ANNIVERSARY

Introduction

As was the case with most major railway companies, the line that in 1839 became the London & South Western Railway was first conceived to join two centres — London and Southampton — of national importance, the remarkable degree of shelter offered by the Solent and Southampton Water having made the latter city ideal for the development of docks.

The original London terminus at Nine Elms lost its passenger service in 1848, when the line was extended to Waterloo. However, it also housed the locomotive, carriage and wagon works. Nine Elms Works would build 806 engines until 1909, when lack of room for expansion would cause closure and transfer of such activities to Eastleigh. The next extension to the LSWR was the 1841 line from Bishopstoke (later Eastleigh) to Gosport. However, it would be another six years before Portsmouth was reached, by virtue of running powers granted over the London, Brighton & South Coast Railway, and 1859 (after lengthy negotiation) before the Portsmouth Direct line was opened. Meanwhile a network of lines was opening up the metropolitan area and spreading throughout Surrey and Hampshire. Salisbury, reached via Bishopstoke in 1847, was afforded direct access

to/from London via Basingstoke 10 years later, this line extending westwards to reach Exeter by 1860.

Further extension to the West Country involved obtaining running powers over the GWR, running eastwards towards Cowley Bridge Junction, Exeter, with down LSWR trains using the GWR up line — an anomaly that was to occur again when the LSWR reached Plymouth. Thus was gained access to North Devon and Cornwall, where the coming of the railway brought about the transformation of fishing ports into holiday resorts — fine while it lasted, but stations were not always in easy reach, and in the 20th century passenger traffic was reduced as omnibus services (with cheaper fares) improved. In any case, such traffic was largely seasonal, and private cars were increasingly carrying residents as well as tourists. Freight traffic was also lost to the road; at one time, for example, Padstow had a thriving fish traffic. Callington, Ilfracombe and Sidmouth were examples of branch-line termini accessible only after a lengthy climb up a steep hill, and many of the intermediate stations were just as badly sited in relation to the communities they served. The Beeching axe spared three branches — Exeter–Exmouth, Exeter–Barnstaple and Bere

Front cover: Drummond Class T9 4-4-0 No 30719 pauses at Tower Hill on the 9.56am Oakhampton–Padstow, 15 July 1960. The guard consults his watch as time is spent waiting for No 34110 *66 Squadron* to pass on the 9.33am Padstow portion of the up 'Atlantic Coast Express'. Tower Hill was the last station in Devon on the North Cornwall line and was demolished after closure in 1966. *R. C. Riley*

Back cover: The last Beattie well tank built, No 30586 (SR No 3329) of 1875, differed from the other two survivors in having square splashers. It was normally on shunting duties at Wadebridge but from time to time replaced an Adams 'O2' 0-4-4T on lightly loaded trains to Bodmin or Padstow. It was recorded on 15 July 1960. *R. C. Riley*

Title page: In the hands of Adams 'Radial' 4-4-2T No 30583, the first train of the day (13 July 1960) from Axminster to Lyme Regis hardly looks well patronised as it approaches Combpyne. *R. C. Riley*

First published 2002

ISBN 0 7110 2893 1

Published by Ian Allan Publishing

an imprint of Ian Allan Publishing Ltd, Hersham, Surrey KT12 4RG.
Printed by Ian Allan Printing Ltd, Hersham, Surrey KT12 4RG.

Code: 0211/B2

Alston–Gunnislake — the latter's line from Plymouth having once been part of the LSWR main line to Exeter. In addition, the line from Exeter to Okehampton would survive in order to serve Meldon Quarry.

The change of regional boundary when the WR took control in 1963 had an even more damaging effect. That seaside branches would close was inevitable, but it was unnecessary to single the ex-LSWR main line from Salisbury to Exeter, while the main line thence to Plymouth could have served as an alternative route at times when the ex-GWR line past Dawlish was suffering from its proximity to the sea.

East of Salisbury there have been just as many branch closures, although the LSWR's electrification policy, continued by the Southern Railway, was responsible for saving much of the old infrastructure. However, it was not until 1967 that the third rail reached Bournemouth, this being the last steam-operated main line on the Southern Region.

This book is intended to show something of the LSWR and SR locomotives, rolling stock and infrastructure as they were in the BR era in the 1950s and '60s.

Acknowledgements

Acknowledgement is given to all the photographers whose work appears in this book, as well as to Marjorie Fisher for use of the transparencies from the late G. W. Powell. Thanks also to Peter Waller and his colleagues at Ian Allan Publishing Ltd and to my wife, Christine.

While the original Bulleid Pacifics were marvellous engines, they had their faults, not least of which was that they were not economical in service. It was resolved that the 'Merchant Navys' should be rebuilt to BR design standards as far as possible, and the 30 engines of this class were rebuilt thus between 1956 and 1959. Without the so-called 'air-smoothed' sideplates they looked handsome and powerful machines. They were given names representing shipping lines that used Southampton Docks in peacetime, the first reflecting the SR's own maritime activities; No 35001 *Channel Packet* was recorded on the down 'Bournemouth Belle' at Clapham Junction on 13 September 1959. This Pullman train was inaugurated in 1931, restored in 1946 after wartime closure and withdrawn in 1967 following electrification. *R. C. Riley*

Above: The first 10 of the 'Merchant Navy' class were built at Eastleigh in 1941/2, materials for their construction having been ordered before the outbreak of war in 1939. With their 6ft 2in wheels they were initially described as mixed-traffic engines, and in fact during the war, with five at Nine Elms and five at Salisbury, they were used on the heaviest freight trains to Exeter and Southampton. Twenty more were delivered between 1944 and 1949 and, as passenger services were augmented and accelerated with the onset of peace, they took their place as express passenger locomotives. Most were in black livery in wartime, soon to give way to malachite green from 1945. The newly nationalised BR decided in 1949 that the top express engines should be painted dark blue. Two years later this decision was revoked and Brunswick green was chosen. No 35007 *Aberdeen Commonwealth* was in blue livery from 1950 to 1952 and was recorded at Nine Elms on 16 September 1950. *G. W. Powell*

Right: There were no fewer than 105 members of Drummond's 'M7' class built between 1897 and 1911. Initially employed on semi-fast main-line work, they took over the London suburban services and similar work elsewhere after derailment of one near Tavistock in 1898 brought criticism by the Board of Trade. Nevertheless they still carried out stopping passenger work over quite long distances, but from 1915 the LSWR commenced electrification, and this policy continued under the SR, including even the main line to Portsmouth. After the World War 2 years of black livery it was a refreshing change to see six of the 'M7s' repainted in malachite green between 1946 and 1948, these being employed on Waterloo empty-stock workings. Of these, No 30038 was recorded on Nine Elms shed, 4 March 1950. This colourful practice was not continued in BR days. *G. W. Powell*

Left: The Maunsell 'King Arthur' class was developed from the Urie-designed 'N15' built between 1918 and 1923. The modernisation of these engines was the work of the talented design team Maunsell had built up at Ashford. Ten engines (Nos 448-57) were built at Eastleigh in 1925, while a further 30 (Nos 763-92) were delivered concurrently from the North British Locomotive Co. This latter batch had a modified cab in order to work on ex-SECR lines. A final series of 14 (Nos 793-806) emerged from Eastleigh with six-wheeled tenders, enabling them to work on ex-LBSC lines, where turntable lengths were restrictive.
  John Elliot, SR Public Relations Assistant, had the happy inspiration of choosing names from Arthurian Legend for these engines. No 30453 *King Arthur*, recorded at Nine Elms on 6 September 1958, would achieve a final mileage of over two million miles. *R. C. Riley*

Above: R. W. Urie, Chief Mechanical Engineer 1912-22, designed three classes of 4-6-0 — the 'H15' class with 6ft 0in coupled wheels, the 'N15s' with 6ft 7in coupled wheels and the 'S15s' with 5ft 7in coupled wheels. With their high running-plates and easy accessibility to the motion they were a considerable contrast to their Drummond predecessors. Twenty 'S15s' (Nos 496-515) were built in 1920/1. Originally fitted with stovepipe chimneys, they had replacements of Class U1 design fitted during World War 2, improving their appearance. No 30511 was recorded on a down main-line empty-stock train to Southampton Docks at Vauxhall, 20 June 1959. *R. C. Riley*

Left: The handsome Class H16 4-6-2Ts of 1921/2 (Nos 516-20) were intended to work interchange freight trains between Feltham and Brent or Willesden, their appearance coinciding with the opening of the extensive marshalling yard at Feltham. In SR days, when they made appearances on Ascot Race Specials, they were painted in green passenger livery. In wartime they carried the inevitable black livery and remained thus postwar. In BR days, as traffic increased, they were often to be seen on empty-stock trains between Clapham Junction and Waterloo. Unusually No 30519 was recorded at Clapham Junction with a shunter's truck, more commonly attached one of the LSWR Class 02 0-4-4Ts or LBSC 'E4' 0-6-2Ts usually entrusted with shunting the extensive (49-road) sidings. *K. W. Wightman*

Below left: Class M7 0-4-4T No 30321 approaching Clapham Junction with empty carriages of Bulleid design. The signalbox, Clapham Junction A, was one of two over-line gantry 'boxes. This one suffered a partial collapse due to metal fatigue in 1965, causing much traffic disruption. These signalboxes have now been superseded by the signalling centre at Wimbledon. *K. W. Wightman*

Below: On a Summer Saturday working, Class S15 No 30501 heads the 3.54pm Waterloo–Basingstoke, 20 June 1959. On such an occasion it was not unusual for Feltham shed to provide motive power to assist Nine Elms. *R. C. Riley*

The Class G16 4-8-0Ts (Nos 492-5) were introduced in 1921 in readiness for their duties 'hump-shunting' at the new gravitation sorting sidings at Feltham, then nearing completion. As was the case with the similar Urie 4-6-2Ts, they were initially shedded at Strawberry Hill pending completion of the new Feltham shed. Like the 4-6-2Ts they were also used on inter-regional freight trains. In 1954 Nos 30494/5 found unusual employment, being loaned for a week to test a new type of bridge on the Hollywater Loop line of the Longmoor Military Railway; the 4-8-0Ts came off best in the trials, the new bridge being abandoned! Displaced by diesels, the 4-8-0Ts and 4-6-2Ts were withdrawn in 1962. No 30495 was recorded on Feltham shed, 17 October 1959. *R. C. Riley*

William Adams was Chief Mechanical Engineer from 1878 to 1895. He had a considerable influence on locomotive design, being best remembered for the 4-4-0 'High Flyers', the 'Jubilee' 0-4-2s and the 'Radial' 4-4-2Ts. At the other end of the scale he designed the powerful 'B4' 0-4-0Ts and 'G6' 0-6-0Ts. The latter first appeared in 1894, and by 1900 there were 34 of these shunting engines in service, allocated throughout the system. All were built at Nine Elms Works, the later engines during Drummond's tenure as CME. Of these, 1900-built No 30349 was recorded at Feltham shed on 19 March 1961, four months before withdrawal. *R. C. Riley*

Above: On the death of Dugald Drummond, Robert Urie was appointed CME. Although Drummond's 4-4-0s were fine machines, his 26 4-6-0s were a disaster. Urie soon addressed this problem with three strongly built classes of 4-6-0, so that virtually within a decade from 1914 there were 66 of these in service, with more to follow with modifications by Maunsell in SR days. The express-passenger version was the 'N15' class, of which 20 were originally built; when Maunsell built a further 54, some alterations were made to the Urie engines, notably in the blastpipe design. When John Elliot, Assistant to the General Manager, chose names from Arthurian legend, the Urie 'N15s' were included. Having arrived from Waterloo, No 30745 *Tintagel* stands in Basingstoke shed yard, 12 September 1954. *G. W. Powell*

Right: Leaving Basingstoke under one of the familiar LSWR gantry signals, Class U 2-6-0 No 31806 heads a train for Portsmouth. This engine was originally one of the 20 'River' class 2-6-4Ts built in 1925/6 following trials with the prototype engine (SECR No 790) of 1917. In this form these engines never ran on LSWR lines, where their water capacity would have proved insufficient. In August 1927 No A800 was derailed at speed near Sevenoaks, resulting in some loss of life. The engines were immediately withdrawn from service, and, after trials indicated that their rough riding gave cause for concern, all were converted to (nameless) tender engines in 1928; No 31806 had less than a year of active life in its original form as *River Torridge*. Subsequently 30 more Class U engines were built, and, apart from a handful at Redhill or Reading, all were allocated to former LSWR sheds. One of the 'Rivers', No A890, was a three-cylinder version, and upon rebuilding this became the prototype Class U1 engine. *K. W. Wightman*

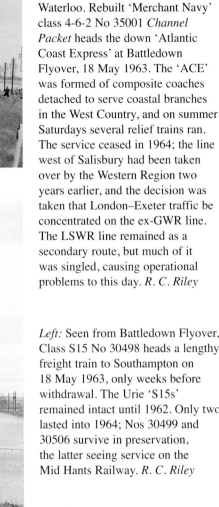

Left: In anticipation of the main line between Woking and Worting Junction (west of Basingstoke) becoming four-tracked, the up Bournemouth line crossed the Exeter lines on the new Battledown Flyover built in 1897. The track-widening was completed in 1904, thereby providing four tracks throughout to Waterloo. Rebuilt 'Merchant Navy' class 4-6-2 No 35001 *Channel Packet* heads the down 'Atlantic Coast Express' at Battledown Flyover, 18 May 1963. The 'ACE' was formed of composite coaches detached to serve coastal branches in the West Country, and on summer Saturdays several relief trains ran. The service ceased in 1964; the line west of Salisbury had been taken over by the Western Region two years earlier, and the decision was taken that London–Exeter traffic be concentrated on the ex-GWR line. The LSWR line remained as a secondary route, but much of it was singled, causing operational problems to this day. *R. C. Riley*

Left: Seen from Battledown Flyover, Class S15 No 30498 heads a lengthy freight train to Southampton on 18 May 1963, only weeks before withdrawal. The Urie 'S15s' remained intact until 1962. Only two lasted into 1964; Nos 30499 and 30506 survive in preservation, the latter seeing service on the Mid Hants Railway. *R. C. Riley*

Right: The four-mile branch from Bentley to Bordon was opened in 1905 at the behest of the War Office in order to serve the then new Woolmer Instructional Military Railway, later better known as the Longmoor Military Railway. The line was usually worked by Class M7 0-4-4Ts on a pull-and-push train, but on 4 October 1958 Drummond Class T9 4-4-0 No 30120 visited Bordon on a railtour organised by the RCTS. This engine survives in the National Collection and is currently awaiting overhaul on the Bluebell Railway. The Bordon branch lost its passenger traffic in 1957, the freight following nine years later. *R. C. Riley*

Right: A tranquil scene at Medstead & Four Marks on Sunday 8 May 1955 as Class M7 0-4-4T No 30480 pauses with a Winchester–Alton train. At the time trains, including a 'Merchant Navy' on the 'Bournemouth Belle', were being diverted over this route because of engineering works on the main line. The so-named Mid Hants line lasted long enough to be served by diesel-electric multiple-units, but the service was withdrawn in 1973. The line between Alton and Alresford survives in preservation. *R. C. Riley*

Left: The sturdy Adams 0-4-0Ts of Class B4 were introduced in 1891 for service at Devonport Docks and on station pilot duties. In the event the LSWR acquired Southampton Docks in 1892. By 1908 there were 25 engines in service, of which 13 were allocated to Southampton Docks. Apart from *Jersey, Guernsey* and *Alderney* they carried French names, but these were removed after the war when 14 surplus USA Transportation Corps 0-6-0Ts were bought for use at Southampton Docks. Apart from those 'B4s' at Plymouth, Bournemouth had four (two of which worked from Hamworthy) and Eastleigh three. Of those based at Eastleigh, one was outshedded at Winchester for yard pilot duties. No 30093, formerly *St Malo*, was performing this duty on 5 March 1960. *R. C. Riley*

Above: In 1903 Nine Elms turned out two steam railmotors for the branch from Fratton to East Southsea, worked jointly with the LBSCR. There followed a few more to work on unremunerative branch lines. Finally thoughts turned to railmotor engines separated from the coach. As 2-2-0Ts these were feeble machines, and all but three were sold to Government agencies in World War 1. The survivors were rebuilt as 0-4-0Ts, two sharing duties at Southampton Royal Pier, the third shunting Redbridge Sleeper Works. Class C14 0-4-0T No 30588 was recorded at Southampton, 26 June 1957. Both Southampton engines were withdrawn in 1957, being replaced by the Redbridge engine, which survived for two more years. *R. C. Riley*

Left: On 24 June 1957 Maunsell 'King Arthur' 4-6-0 No 30781 *Sir Aglovale* approaches Winchester City at the head of a Bournemouth–Birkenhead train, which it will work as far as Oxford. No 30781 was of the 1925 series (Nos 763-92) built by the North British Locomotive Co. *R. C. Riley*

Above: Apart from the two 'Britannia' 4-6-2s allocated to Stewarts Lane in 1951, the BR Class 4 2-6-0s were the first standard engines in any

number to reach the SR. Apart from some at Redhill they were mostly at South Western Sheds, Eastleigh having the largest number. Having been delayed by the passage of an up 'Ocean Liner Express', No 76067 prepares to leave Winchester City with the 6.35am Bournemouth Central–Basingstoke stopping train, 24 June 1957. Remarkably, ex-SECR Class P 0-6-0T No 31325 was on short-term loan as yard pilot in place of the usual, more powerful 'B4' 0-4-0T. *R. C. Riley*

Left: In 1955 10 BR Class 5 4-6-0s (Nos 73110-9) were allocated to Nine Elms. In 1959 the Kent Coast electrification released 12 from Stewarts Lane, and in the early 1960s more arrived, having been displaced from other regions. These in turn displaced the Maunsell express-passenger engines, while the anticipation of elimination of steam from the SR in 1967 led to a reduction in repairs. Hence engines were stopped and replaced often by equally run-down machines from other regions. No 73110, in grimy condition, was recorded at Micheldever on a down van train, 18 June 1966. Nos 73080-9, 73110-9 carried the names of withdrawn 'King Arthurs'. *D. B. Clark*

Above: Bulleid Light Pacific No 34023 *Blackmore Vale* was scheduled for private preservation, hence its apparent pristine condition when seen near Salisbury on 5 June 1967, only a month before the end of SR steam; the nameplate had been removed for safe-keeping. There were 110 of these engines, with 'West Country' or 'Battle of Britain' names, built 1945-51, of which 60 were rebuilt 1957-61 along similar lines to the 'Merchant Navys'. *D. B. Clark*

Above: Maunsell 'King Arthur' 4-6-0 No 30770 *Sir Prianius* nears completion of overhaul in the Erecting Shop at Eastleigh Works, 25 August 1957. This locomotive would be the last of the class to be withdrawn, in November 1962. *R. C. Riley*

Right: Newly overhauled 'Lord Nelson' 4-6-0 No 30851 *Sir Francis Drake* stands outside Eastleigh Works, 4 September 1954. Bulleid had improved these locomotives with Lemaitre chimneys and redesigned cylinders, in which condition they proved reliable engines. *G. W. Powell*

24

Left: During William Adams' tenure as CME the standard 0-6-0 goods engine was the '0395' class, of which 70 were built from 1881 to 1886. In 1903 they were placed on the duplicate list, and during World War 1 no fewer than 50 were sold to the War Department for service in the Middle East. Nevertheless 18 survived to be taken into BR stock for shunting and light goods duties. Repainted at Eastleigh on 4 September 1954, No 30567 of Feltham shed was the last to be withdrawn, five years later. *G. W. Powell*

Above: The '700' class 0-6-0 freight engines, 30 of which were built in 1897, had many features in common with the Class M7 0-4-4Ts. No 30368 was recorded at Eastleigh shed equipped for snowplough duties; engines of this class were also based at Exmouth Junction, where they were similarly fitted, as was necessary for lines skirting Dartmoor. The class was officially withdrawn at the end of 1962, but, in view of the wintry conditions that prevailed in the early months of 1963, a 'blind eye' was turned to their continuing vital work with the snowploughs. *D. B. Clark*

As already mentioned, Urie set his stamp on locomotive design with his three sturdy 4-6-0 classes. The first 10 (Nos 482-91) entered service in 1914 and proved a great asset in meeting the increased demands of wartime traffic. This 'H15' mixed-traffic class was augmented by the rebuilding of six Drummond 4-6-0s (Nos 330-5), while the SR added 10 more in 1924. On 26 June 1957 No 30473, first of the SR batch, prepares to enter Southampton Docks, host to two Cunard liners — the RMS *Queen Mary* and RMS *Ivernia*. Southampton Terminus station can be glimpsed under the road overbridge. *R. C. Riley*

Before World War 2 the 'Lord Nelsons' were shared between Nine Elms and Stewarts Lane, but with the cessation of Continental services the 16 engines were all concentrated on ex-LSWR lines. With the abundance of Bulleid Pacifics, they fitted in on Bournemouth-line duties and 'Ocean Liner' expresses to/from Southampton Docks. No 30857 *Lord Howe* was heading for the Docks on a Greek Line special, 26 June 1957. *R. C. Riley*

27

Above: A parade of Southampton Docks shunting engines, led by ex-LBSC Class E1 0-6-0T No 32113 and ex-USA Transportation Corps 0-6-0T No 30061. Behind can be seen ex-LBSC Class E2 0-6-0T No 32109 and another 'E1', No 32689. Note the boxes on the cab roof which housed a short-wave radio system. The building of these engines covered the years 1877 to 1942. *K. W. Wightman*

Right: Rebuilt Bulleid Light Pacific No 34014 *Budleigh Salterton* leaves Southampton Central with the Brighton–Bournemouth train, 1 July 1962. Note the varied carriage liveries at this time. This locomotive's nameplate was unusual, the long name being spread over two lines. *D. B. Clark*

Left: An intriguing shot of Class T9 4-4-0 No 30707 at Brockenhurst, 15 August 1959, with headcode for Bournemouth via Wimborne and the 'Old Road'. The train, probably the 9.32am to Wimborne, consists of two ex-LSWR non-corridor coaches in differing liveries. This combination normally indicated non-availability of a motor-fitted 'M7' or carriage set. No 30707 acquired a six-wheeled tender — a feature normally associated with engines loaned to ex-SECR lines in prewar and immediate postwar years — from a '700'-class 0-6-0 in 1955 and was the last 'T9' to receive a general overhaul at Eastleigh, in March 1959. *G. W. Powell*

Above: Drummond 'M7' class 0-4-4T No 30328, with its push-and-pull set augmented by a suitably fitted SECR Third, stands at Brockenhurst between duties on 15 August 1959. The 'M7s' covered most of the duties to Bournemouth West via Wimborne and Ringwood, known as the 'Old Road' because it was opened in 1847; the direct route via Sway to Christchurch and thence Bournemouth was not built until 1888. Use of 'M7s' on push-and-pull work ceased in 1964. *G. W. Powell*

Left: There was a daily freight turn from Bevois Park to Lymington which did the necessary shunting at Brockenhurst. On 28 June 1957 Maunsell Class Q 0-6-0 No 30531 was appropriately in charge. The engine was turned on the turntable at Brockenhurst in readiness for its return journey so that the only tender-first running was thence to Lymington Town. *R. C. Riley*

Above: A less appropriate choice of motive power often used at this time was a Drummond Class T9 4-4-0, on this occasion No 30289. Known as 'Greyhounds', the 66 'T9s', built 1899-1901, were the main express-passenger engines of their day, regularly achieving speeds in the 80s. Withdrawal took place between 1951 and 1961. *R. C. Riley*

Above left: Rebuilt 'Merchant Navy' No 35001 *Channel Packet* heads a Weymouth–Waterloo express on the approach to Bournemouth Central during 1962. In the siding beside the engine shed, the station pilot, Class M7 0-4-4T No 30112, waits with the coaches from Bournemouth West. In 1938, when the writer made this journey, the pilot was an Adams 'Jubilee' 0-4-2 and the train engine a 'Lord Nelson'. *C. P. Boocock*

Left: The station pilot now propels the Bournemouth West portion onto the train. The carriage set —No 292, of Bulleid design — was one of 11

built for the Bournemouth line in 1947. The train engine from the West station (closed 1965) would have been a tender-first Bulleid Pacific from an earlier arrival. *C. P. Boocock*

Above: 'Merchant Navy' class 4-6-2 No 35012 *United States Lines* heads the up 'Bournemouth Belle' at the Central station, 24 May 1959. In 2001 the station was restored to its former glory following thorough cleaning of its brickwork and re-glazing of its overall roof. *C. P. Boocock*

Above: In the months leading up to the July 1967 electrification some ex-LNER Pacifics visited the South Western. On 3 June preserved Class A4 No 4498 *Sir Nigel Gresley* was recorded on an up charter special at Bournemouth Central. *R. C. Riley*

Right: Displaced at Brighton by diesel units, 2-6-4T No 80146 approaches Swanage with a train from Wareham, 4 June 1966.

The Swanage branch was opened in 1885. Having lost its freight traffic in 1965 and although worked by DEMUs, it was quite wrongly closed altogether seven years later. Fortunately a preservation society stepped in and now operates the line from Swanage to Norden. A portion of the line from the Worgret Junction end serves an oil terminal at Furzebrook, but it is hoped that the Swanage Railway may one day return to Wareham. *R. C. Riley*

Left: Bulleid 'West Country' class No 34105 *Swanage* heads the 1.25pm Weymouth–Waterloo at Dorchester South, 10 July 1956. The 1847 line of the Southampton & Dorchester Railway ran via Brockenhurst, Ringwood, Wimborne and Wareham, with its terminus at what became the LSWR station at Dorchester ('South' being added in BR days). The 1857 mixed-gauge extension to Weymouth curved round with a down platform, but up trains had to pass the terminus and reverse back into the platform. This practice continued until after the 1967 dieselisation from Bournemouth to Weymouth (later to be electrified). *R. C. Riley*

Above: A powerful shot of rebuilt 'Merchant Navy' No 35001 *Channel Packet* on an express to Waterloo at Dorchester South, 1 September 1964. *G. W. Powell*

Left: The ex-LSWR engine shed at Dorchester closed in 1957, after which the former GWR shed at Weymouth was used. There had also been a small LSWR engine shed at Weymouth, notably for Adams 0-4-4Ts used on the Portland branch; this closed in 1939. Urie Class S15 No 30498, with only nine months to withdrawal, runs light from the ex-GWR shed to work an up freight on 4 October 1962. *C. L. Caddy*

Above: At the top of Bincombe Bank, 'Merchant Navy' 4-6-2 No 35030 *Elder Dempster Lines* heads a Weymouth–Waterloo boat train, 12 June 1967. Remarkably clean for an engine to be withdrawn in less than a month, it has had its nameplate removed into safe custody. Thanks to a diesel failure, it would work the last steam-hauled Weymouth–Waterloo express, on 9 July 1967. *R. C. Riley*

'West Country' class 4-6-2 No 34091 *Weymouth* is seen near Romsey
in charge of a Salisbury–Portsmouth train. In its years at Stewarts Lane,
prior to completion of the Kent Coast electrification, this was one of the
Pacifics chosen to work the 'Golden Arrow'. *K. W. Wightman*

BR Class 4MT No 76062 heads in the opposite direction on a Portsmouth–
Salisbury train. Although Eastleigh shed gained its first 15 '4MT' 2-6-0s in
1953, with the SR allocation later increasing by a further 17, no fewer than
13 Drummond 'T9' 4-4-0s survived until 1961. *K. W. Wightman*

Left: For many years pull-and-push-fitted Drummond 'M7' 0-4-4Ts Nos 30129 and 30131 shared the working of the Yeovil Town–Yeovil Junction service. With just over a year left in service, No 30129 stands at Yeovil Town on 6 October 1962. *R. C. Riley*

Below: Proving its mixed-traffic abilities, 'Battle of Britain' 4-6-2 No 34069 *Hawkinge* pauses to take water at Yeovil Junction on a down freight working, 22 July 1958. The station is now but a shadow of its former self; weekday connection to the town is by means of a bus service. *R. C. Riley*

Above: Between 1903 and 1906 the LSWR was an early pioneer in the use of steam railcars. Realising that these lacked flexibility, it next tried small 2-2-0Ts with purpose-built trailer cars. Within a few years the carriage portions were rebuilt as orthodox railmotor trailers. Access doors were of decorative ironwork, hence these two-car sets' becoming known as the 'gate stock'. The series was followed by three new sets in 1914, the last of which, Set 373, was recorded at Yeovil Junction, 10 July 1959. It survived until October 1960. *R. C. Riley*

Right: The SR, following the example of the LSWR, was adept at converting suburban steam stock for electric use. It also placed old carriages on new, extended underframes, adding new compartments as required. Pull-and-push set No 1 consisted of a driving composite 56ft coach of 1911 and a 58ft Third coach of 1898 origin extended on a new underframe in 1936. *G. W. Powell*

Maunsell 'S15' class 4-6-0 No 30823 heads a Salisbury–Exeter stopping train out of Seaton Junction, 13 July 1963. This was at a time when trials were made over the Seaton branch with ex-GWR auto-fitted engines and railmotor trailers, on this occasion 0-6-0PT No 6430.

This was a short-lived side-effect of BR Regional Boundary changes in 1963, when SR lines west of Salisbury were transferred to the WR. A controversial result was that much of the former main line to Exeter was singled. *R. C. Riley*

An up pick-up freight pauses at Broad Clyst, the location of a Civil Engineers' depot, on 6 July 1961. No 30824 was one of a batch of 15 'S15s' built in 1927/8, to be followed by a further series of 10 engines in 1936. Useful engines, some survived into 1965, by which time the WR had inflicted its short-lived diesel-hydraulic locomotives on the line. *R. C. Riley*

Left: A rebuilt 'Merchant Navy', No 35022 *Holland America Line*, at speed on the approach to Seaton Junction with the up 'Atlantic Coast Express', 4 September 1962. Precisely two years later this engine would head the last down 'ACE' — an exhilarating run as a tribute to the end of SR steam to the West. *G. W. Powell*

Above: The 'West Country' class carried BR numbers 34001-48 and 34091-108. Those engines carrying 'Battle of Britain' names were in the series 34049-90, 34109/10. The penultimate engine of the class, No 34109 *Sir Trafford Leigh Mallory*, makes a powerful impression in rebuilt form at Seaton Junction, 9 September 1961. *G. W. Powell*

Above: Push-and-pull-fitted Class M7 0-4-4T No 30048 pauses at Colyton on a branch train to Seaton, 14 July 1960. In 1959/60 the SR converted 20 Maunsell Brake Composites and Open Seconds (Sets 600-619) for push-and-pull use, Set 603 being seen here. The branch and Seaton Junction station were closed in 1966. This end of the line is now the home of Seaton & District Electric Tramway, of 2ft 9in gauge, operated as a leisure line in the summer months. *R. C. Riley*

Right: The signalman at Sidmouth stands ready to pick up the single-line tablet covering the section from Tipton St Johns, 24 July 1958. Class M7 0-4-4T No 30044 was not push-and-pull-fitted and was heading corridor coaches. A visit a year later found the line in the hands of the popular Ivatt '2MT' 2-6-2Ts and the less favoured BR Class 3MT 2-6-2Ts. There was little local traffic, the station only being accessible a mile up a steep hill. The line closed in 1967. *R. C. Riley*

Left: The Axminster–Lyme Regis line was opened in 1903 under a Light Railway Order. It had some sharp curves, and initially the LSWR bought two Stroudley 'Terrier' 0-6-0Ts to work it, but, as traffic grew, Adams Class O2 0-4-4Ts — with side tanks only half-full, to reduce the weight — replaced them in 1907. These engines proving less than successful, trials were carried out with one-time London suburban Adams 'Radial' 4-4-2Ts of 1885. With modified side play to the bogies to aid smooth riding on the curves, these engines took over branch working in 1913. At Axminster on 11 July 1959, No 30584 was in the process of shunting Bulleid set No 970 — through coaches from the 8.05am Waterloo. This movement could not be completed until the two-coach branch train arrived. The two 'Radial' tanks would then double-head the combined train to Lyme Regis. *R. C. Riley*

Below: There were no domestic coal merchants about, so the photographer was able to gain sufficient height to catch a glimpse of the sea at Lyme Regis; like Sidmouth, the station was high above the town. By 1925 only two 'Radial' tanks survived, and in 1946 the opportunity came to acquire a third, which had been sold to the Ministry of Munitions in 1917 and was now standing derelict on the East Kent Railway. In BR days this became No 30583, seen at Lyme Regis on 14 July 1960. Two months later an Ivatt '2MT' 2-6-2T was successfully tried on the line. These duly took over, but, after a brief spell of dieselisation, the branch closed in 1965. No 30583 survives on the Bluebell Railway, however. *R. C. Riley*

Left: One branch to survive the WR closures was that between Exeter and Exmouth. Not only did it employ BR standard engines — Class 3MT 2-6-2Ts — but it also used BR suburban-type non-corridor coaches, built in 1955. No 82025 runs alongside the River Exe on the approach to Exmouth, 13 October 1959. *R. C. Riley*

Above: Ivatt Class 2MT No 41318 enters Exmouth with the 2.49pm from Exeter Central on 13 October 1959. At that time the station had four platforms, one of which had run-round facilities, and a half-hourly service; it has since been reduced to one platform of reduced length. The small engine shed was closed in 1963. *R. C. Riley*

The engine shed at Exmouth Junction was totally rebuilt in early SR days and could boast an allocation of around 130 engines, some of which were allocated among its seven outstations. It was the largest locomotive depot on former LSWR lines. At one time its allocation included 30 of the 'N' class Moguls, but this number was halved in postwar years with the arrival in quantity of Bulleid Pacifics. Entering the shed yard past the six-road carriage & wagon repair depot on 5 July 1957, No 30331 was one of six engines rebuilt as Class H15s from unsuccessful Drummond 4-6-0s. This large site also housed an Engineer's depot and the concrete works established in 1913 which could supply anything from a milepost to a locomotive depot. *R. C. Riley*

Before the advent of the Bulleid Pacifics, all main-line services west of Exeter were handled by 'T9' class 4-4-0s or 'N' class 2-6-0s, as portrayed by Nos 30313 and 31845 standing outside Exmouth Junction shed, 5 July 1961. Note the concrete buildings. No 30313 was one of the last series of 'T9s' built at Nine Elms Works in 1900: these had wider cabs and splashers. One of the last survivors, it was due to make its last journey to Eastleigh the following day. *R. C. Riley*

Left: 'West Country' 4-6-2 No 34023 *Blackmore Vale* heads a Plymouth–Waterloo express joining the former GWR *down* main line at Cowley Bridge Junction, Exeter, on 16 July 1958. Two months later the LSWR terminus at Plymouth Friary was closed, to be followed 10 years later by the main line between Meldon Quarry and Bere Alston. *R. C. Riley*

Above: At the same location, 'West Country' 4-6-2 No 34096 *Trevone* heads a down (Ilfracombe) express, 16 July 1960. The usual anomaly of Cowley Bridge applies: the train is traversing the ex-GWR up line. The SR line westwards, now singled, serves only Barnstaple and Meldon Quarry. *R. C. Riley*

In the 1960s some non-passenger traffic remained, apart from Meldon Quarry ballast. Class M7 0-4-4T No 30670 heads the Crediton milk train, 6 July 1961. At Exeter St Davids the tanks went eastwards via the WR route on the 12.20pm Penzance–Kensington milk train. *R. C. Riley*

'West Country' class 4-6-2 No 34029 *Lundy*, stopped by GWR
semaphore signals, stands waiting for the road at Cowley Bridge
Junction on 16 July 1958. This was the up Bideford meat train.
R. C. Riley

Below: In 1929 Brighton Works turned out eight three-cylinder heavy-shunting engines (Nos 950-7), of which two were allocated to ex-LSWR sheds. In 1956 two were tried as bankers between Exeter St Davids and Exeter Central. At this time the WR Civil Engineer would not sanction their use; three years later this ban was removed, but the 0-8-0Ts were replaced in 1962 by 'W' class 2-6-4Ts. No 30952 was on pilot duties at Exeter Central on 6 July 1961. *R. C. Riley*

Right: Between 1927 and 1929 10 ex-LBSC Stroudley 'E1' 0-6-0Ts were rebuilt as 0-6-2Ts, with lengthened frames to accommodate a larger bunker. They were divided between Exmouth Junction and Barnstaple; at the latter shed their duties included the Torrington & Halwill line. In 1938 these 'E1/Rs' replaced 'G6' class 0-6-0Ts on the banking duties at Exeter; it was worth a night or two in a hotel near St Davids station, if only to hear the mellow Stroudley whistles as they went about their banking work. These remarkable little engines were built between 1874 and 1883, and the last was not withdrawn until 1959. Here Nos 32695 and 32135 await their next turn of duty in the banker's siding at St Davids, 20 July 1956. *R. C. Riley*

Devonport King's Road suffered severe damage from enemy action in World War 2. Standing in the up platform on 30 August 1961 is rebuilt 'West Country' No 34104 *Bere Alston* with the 2.25pm all-stations train from Plymouth to Exeter Central. The LSWR terminus at Plymouth Friary had closed in 1958, after which SR trains began their journey at North Road WR station. By then in WR ownership, Devonport King's Road would close in 1964. *R. C. Riley*

Rounding the curve at Mount Gould Junction, Plymouth, is another rebuilt 'West Country' — No 34097 *Holsworthy* — with the empty carriages to form the Sunday-morning Waterloo express from Plymouth North Road, 9 July 1961. The train was formed in Laira carriage sidings by 'O2' class 0-4-4T No 30225. *R. C. Riley*

Above: Adams 'O2' class 0-4-4T No 30192 shunting the sidings at Devonport, 3 May 1961. At this time there were still four 'O2s' at Plymouth Friary shed, their retention dictated by the sharp curves of the most-weekdays trip over the Stonehouse Pool branch. Class 04 diesels had already replaced the 'B4' 0-4-0Ts, and by the end of 1962 the last 'O2s' on the mainland had also gone, although a few would remain on the much truncated Isle of Wight system until 1966. *R. C. Riley*

Right: The North Devon & Cornwall Junction Railway was built under a Light Railway Order and was opened in July 1925. Its Consulting Engineer was Colonel H. F. Stephens, doyen of the light-railway movement. Initially motive power was provided by 1884-built 4-4-0s of Adams' '0460' class, one-time express engines but with low axle weight. From 1927 they were replaced by equally venerable engines, the rebuilt 'E1/R' 0-6-2Ts. In 1953 LMR Ivatt 2-6-2Ts took over until closure of the line in 1965. No 41312 plus a Bulleid composite brake form the 8.52am Torrington–Halwill Junction at Hatherleigh on 25 September 1962. *R. C. Riley*

Left: Minus headboard, 'Battle of Britain' No 34066 *Spitfire* approaches Barnstaple Junction with the Ilfracombe portion of the up 'Atlantic Coast Express' on Saturday 16 June 1962. The line west of Barnstaple Junction survived until 1970 and was the subject of a failed preservation scheme, but, with its 1-in-37 gradient, what a line to work! The line to Torrington closed five years earlier. *R. C. Riley*

Above: 'Battle of Britain' No 34078 *222 Squadron* pauses at North Tawton with a Waterloo–Padstow express, 25 July 1964. The North Cornwall line to Padstow closed in 1967. *R. C. Riley*

Left: At the end of World War 1 consideration was given to keeping munitions workers in employment. One outcome was the decision to build 100 'N' class 2-6-0s at Woolwich Arsenal, boilers being supplied by outside contractors. A lack of skills and adequate supervision meant that 50 kits of parts were bought cheaply by the SR, with assembly taking place at Ashford; these locomotives thus gained the nickname of 'Woolworths'. Around 35 were allocated to ex-LSWR sheds, Nos A826-60 being shared between Salisbury, Exmouth Junction and Barnstaple. Between 1957 and 1961 a number were rebuilt with new or part-new frames and new cylinders with outside steam pipes. No 31837, one of these rebuilds, is seen at Launceston with the 3.13pm Padstow–Exeter Central, 2 May 1961. *R. C. Riley*

Above: The three-cylinder 'U1' 2-6-0s proved less popular than the 'N' and 'U' classes, and this is borne out by their relatively frequent allocation changes. Between 1937 and 1939 Nos 31890-9 were at Exmouth Junction, but, with wartime needs for freight work taking priority, they went to Guildford, replaced by Class T9 4-4-0s, including some with six-wheeled tenders no longer needed at Stewarts Lane. When the last four 'T9s' left Exmouth Junction for withdrawal in July 1961 they were briefly replaced by Nos 31901-4, but the class was taken out of service the following year. No 31902 was recorded near Port Isaac Road on the 3.13pm Padstow–Exeter Central, 12 July 1961. *R. C. Riley*

Above: A short branch ran from Halwill Junction to Bude, the terminus of which is seen here. BR Class 3MT No 82023 stands in the bay platform in rather grimy condition, 16 June 1962. The Bude branch closed in 1966. *R. C. Riley*

Right: The Plymouth, Devonport & South Western Junction Railway afforded independent access to Plymouth, the LSWR always working the line between Lydford and Devonport. However, the PDSWJ independently acquired the 3ft 6in-gauge East Cornwall Minerals Railway, which reopened as a standard-gauge light railway in 1908, and, along with its three Hawthorn Leslie six-coupled tanks, was taken over by the LSWR in 1922. Adams Class O2s took over much of the passenger traffic, shared from 1953 with Ivatt 2-6-2Ts which displaced the local PDSWJ engines withdrawn in the 1950s. No 41316 stands at Gunnislake, present terminus of the line, on 28 August 1961. *R. C. Riley*

Left: Preparing to work to Padstow, Class T9 4-4-0 No 30729 stands at Wadebridge, 22 July 1960. This engine was one of six transferred to Brighton in 1928, for which it was given a six-wheeled tender to make it suitable for small turntables. In fact this engine returned to the former LSWR lines two years later, retaining its smaller tender until withdrawal in 1961. *R. C. Riley*

Above: This photograph of the three Beattie 2-4-0Ts, Nos 30585-7, was very kindly arranged for me by Mr Brown, Shedmaster at Wadebridge, on 21 June 1962. It is quite remarkable that, of the 85 engines of the class built by Beyer Peacock between 1863 and 1875, these three were the only ones to escape withdrawal in the 19th century, having been found suitable for working china-clay trains over the Wenford Bridge mineral line. *R. C. Riley*

Above: Beattie 2-4-0T No 30585 heads the Wenford Bridge freight train leaving Wadebridge, 17 July 1961. It is on the single line to Boscarne Junction, where the Bodmin line diverges. The track on the right is the single line to Launceston. *R. C. Riley*

Right: A glimpse from the footplate of No 30585, giving an impression of the sharply curved and densely wooded Wenford Bridge line, 13 July

1961. Returning from Wenford Bridge, the load was 29 wagons. Replaced by GWR Dock tanks Nos 1367-9, the 2-4-0Ts were withdrawn in 1962, but Nos 30585 and 30587 went out in style, hauling two RCTS/SLS specials between Waterloo and Hampton Court on one of the London suburban routes for which they were designed. These two survive in preservation. *R. C. Riley*

Index of Locations